With warmest wishes
to
Lois McLean, M.D.
October 28, 2001

Roberto Prallela[?]

The Rights of Children in Separation and Divorce

The
Rights
of
Children
in
Separation
and
Divorce

The Essential Handbook for Parents

Robert C. Prall, M.D.

LANDMARK EDITIONS, INC.

P.O. Box 270169   1402 Kansas Avenue   Kansas City, Missouri 64127

International Standard Book Number: 0-933849-78-8

Library of Congress Cataloging-in-Publication Data
Prall, Robert C., 1918-
    The rights of children in separation and divorce :
    the essential handbook for parents /
  Robert C. Prall
      p. cm.
      ISBN 0-933849-78-8 (LIB.BDG. alk. paper)
      1. Children of divorced parents.
      2. Children's rights.
I. Title
HQ777.5 .P73   2000
305.23--dc21   00-027022

Editors: Nancy R. Thatch
        David Melton

Printed in the United States of America

Landmark Editions, Inc.
P.O. Box 270169
1402 Kansas Avenue
Kansas City, Missouri 64127
(816) 241-4919

To Mary Jane, my staunchest supporter and quintessential editorial assistant and proofreader, without whose help this book could not have been written.

And to all of the families, parents, and children who have helped me learn, through the years, what divorce means to children.

ACKNOWLEDGEMENTS

There are many people I wish to thank.

First, it was David and Nancy Melton of Landmark Editions who encouraged me to write this book. When they first saw my outline of "The Rights of Children in Separation and Divorce" that I have been using for many years in my work with families in mediation of divorce, child custody, and visitation issues, they insisted that it should be expanded and published. I wish to thank them for their splendid editorial assistance with the writing and editing of this book.

To the people who have read and reviewed drafts of the book and made suggestions, I wish to express my appreciation. They include: Gemma Ainslie, Ph.D., Ricardo Ainslie, Ph.D., Kelly Ausley-Flores, J.D., Richard Pesikoff, M.D., Deborah L. Richardson, J.D., E. James Anthony, M.D., FRCpsych., Albert J. Solnit, M.D., and Anne Young, and, of course, the one who has read and re-read this manuscript until she could recite it in her sleep, my wife, Mary Jane Prall.

Robert C. Prall, M.D.

ABOUT THE AUTHOR

Robert C. Prall, M.D., has been a Child, Adolescent, and Adult Psychiatrist and Psychoanalyst for more than fifty years. He has worked extensively with families in emotional distress, especially those undergoing separation or divorce.

He graduated from the University of Pennsylvania School of Medicine and had his training in Child Psychiatry at the Child Study Center in Philadelphia. He graduated in Child, Adolescent, and Adult Psychoanalysis from the Philadelphia Psychoanalytic Institute.

He was Professor of Child Psychiatry at various medical schools in Philadelphia for many years and is presently in Austin, Texas, where he is the Senior Psychiatric Consultant to the Austin State Hospital Children's and Adolescent Psychiatric Unit.

Dr. Prall has lectured nationally and worldwide to professional groups on subjects relating to sensible parenting, child development, and the diagnosis and treatment of emotionally disturbed children and their parents. And he has spoken locally to parent groups, P.T.A.'s, churches and synagogues.

He also participated in the Texas State Bar Continuing Education Program on "The Child in Court", for which he wrote the chapter on The Child in Court: The Child Psychiatrist's Perspective for their book. He has closely collaborated with many of the family law specialists in his area who refer some of their most difficult cases to him for help through mediation. Very often, he has been able to help these families avoid the expense and painful experiences of a court trial regarding custody and visitation issues.

He has used the materials he developed on The Rights of Children in Separation and Divorce for many years while working with families in distress. He found it is very helpful if parents consider the rights of their children when they make decisions during and after the process of separation and divorce.

Dr. Prall has five children and three step-children, as well as twelve grandchildren and two great grandchildren. An avid traveler, photographer, and video photographer, he has traveled all over the world and photographed children in many countries.

"Dr. Bob", as he is known to his patients and friends, is a highly respected professional and a truly remarkable and caring person.

INTRODUCTION

Each year in the United States, more than one million children experience their parents' divorce. Because children seem to be so adaptable and resilient, some adults think that young people can readily survive the separation and divorce of their parents. This is not always the case.

In more than fifty years of practice as a child, adolescent, and adult psychiatrist and psychoanalyst, it has become quite clear that parental separation and divorce are major contributors to emotional and behavioral disturbances in children.

Although some children are able to adjust easily to their parents' divorce, others do not survive as well. These children often show up in the offices of psychiatrists, psychologists, and child guidance clinics in need of help.

Even in the best of circumstances, in a home where both parents are loving and caring and really strive to be good parents, the raising of children offers a wide variety of challenges. When parents separate and/or divorce, many of those challenges multiply.

Now, am I saying that parents should never divorce? No, I certainly am not. Many people have sound reasons for getting a divorce. I don't question their reasons or decisions.

In homes where there is constant emotional upheavals and unresolvable differences, it may indeed be better if the parents do separate and divorce -- better for the parents and better for the children.

There is no doubt that divorce is usually much easier if

the couples have no children. People without children can divide their property, sign papers, and go their separate ways.

People with children, however, may divorce each other, but they cannot divorce their children. The emotional and legal ties between parents and children are much stronger and longer lasting.

Regardless of a divorce, parents are still responsible for their children's welfare. Together, the parents must make certain decisions. Will one parent have sole custody of the children or will the parents have joint custody? What will be a fair time-sharing schedule? Who will pay the child support and how much? Who will pay for their children's medical insurance and college education? And who will be responsible to whom, for what, when, where, how, and so on? Agreeing upon and deciding these things may not be easy, but they are necessary.

While it is sometimes difficult to achieve and maintain a successful divorce, it is not impossible. Many people do it, and they do it very well.

In this book, a list of children's rights in separation and divorce is presented. These rights are invaluable because they can help you, as caring parents, to guide your children safely through the mine fields of separation and divorce.

When the rights of your children are sincerely considered and conscientiously observed by you, your ex-spouse, and the other care-taking adults, despite a separation and divorce, your children can develop and maintain healthy self-esteems and strong feelings of self-worth. As a result, you can raise happier, healthier children who have better opportunities to become healthy, happy adults.

For the sake of your children, I urge both parents — the mother and father — to carefully read and thoughtfully consider all of The Rights of Children in Separation and Divorce.

THE RIGHTS OF CHILDREN IN SEPARATION AND DIVORCE

(1)
The Right to Receive the Love and Attention of Both Parents.

For a child to develop a healthy sense of self-esteem and self-confidence, it is essential that he or she feels loved and valued by both parents.

A wholesome early bonding between both parents and a child lays the foundation for the child's healthy psychological development and his or her capacity for appropriate human relationships in the early stages and for later in life. Having close, loving relationships with both parents offers children proper role models to emulate during childhood and for when they, themselves, become adults.

When children lose one parent, it can do terrible things to them. They may actually grieve for the loss of that parent. This leaves a void that can rarely be filled or replaced by another human being. I don't think this is true, I know it is true. Frequently, adolescents who are deprived of a parent's love will run away in attempts to find their missing parent. Some may even spend much of their entire adult lives in search of that parent.

When there is bitterness and resentment at the time of separation or divorce, it is exceedingly common for one parent, either consciously or unconsciously, to try to shut the child off from the other parent. This may be done by interfering with visits and phone calls. Or one parent may try to convince the children not to love the other parent or that the other parent no longer loves them.

Such selfish interference with the child's right to have the love and attention of both parents is inexcusable!

If you really love your child, you will do everything you can to help your child maintain a close, loving relationship with the other parent. If your child loses that good relationship with the other parent, it can leave a major hole in his or her emotional development and self-esteem.

(2)
The Right to Love Both Parents.

It is also essential that children be able to love both parents. Being able to love both a father and a mother helps to form the building blocks for a child's later ability to develop loving relationships with men, women, and children, including one's own spouse and children. Deprivation of the ability to love either parent can lead to gaps in the foundations of later personal relationships.

(3)
The Right to Freely Express
Their Love for Both Parents without
Fear of Antagonizing Either Parent.

It is vitally important to your children that they be allowed, even encouraged, to express their love for one parent without the other parent resenting it or trying to stop it. Fostering this may be one of the most unselfish acts in your life. It may be very difficult to encourage your children to express their love for someone for whom you may have bitter or unkind feelings. But do it for your child. The rewards can be enormous. The alternatives can be devastating.

Especially after a contested divorce or a fierce custody battle, some parents are so angry that they cannot tolerate their children's showing any love or affection for the other parent. Sensing this hostility, often the children begin to hold in their feelings which frequently leads to emotional upsets and behavior problems that may even require professional psychological treatment.

During treatment, children often say to me, "Mommy tells me how mean Daddy is and that I should hate him like she does!" That is a cruel action! Hearing such a statement from a parent can lead a child to have great loyalty conflicts and stress because of the love for both parents.

(4)
The Right to Have Their Parents Continue Their Interest and Attention to the Children During the Divorce Process.

During the divorce process, both parents should be aware that their children are likely to be suffering as much or more anguish than they are experiencing. At this time, children need extra time and special attention from both adults, and they should be given strong reassurance that they are not losing either parent.

Too often, parents become so involved with the divorce process that they have little time or physical or psychological energy left for taking care of the youngsters. But somehow, they must find the time and energy to give their children needed love and attention, including extra hugs and kisses.

(5)
The Right to Know the Truth
about the Reasons for Their Parents' Divorce.

Children invariably worry and wonder about the reasons for their parents' separation and divorce.

When the family is breaking up, the children's school work often suffers. They can't concentrate in school because they are preoccupied with worrying about their parents' divorce. They try to figure out what has happened to their family and why.

Receiving honest answers to their questions about the divorce can help children avoid many anxious days and sleepless nights. It can also keep them from needlessly blaming themselves for the divorce.

(6)
The Right to Know They Are Not
to Blame for the Divorce.

Almost universally, children tend to blame themselves for their parents' separation.

Many times boys and girls whom I have seen in therapy during or after a divorce worry that they have caused the trouble between their parents. They say such things as: "If only I had been nicer to Daddy, maybe he wouldn't have left us"; or "If I had helped Mother more, maybe she would have stayed with us".

It is very important, in fact, imperative, that both parents make it absolutely clear that their children are not in any way to blame for the separation or divorce!

Tell your children, "The divorce is our fault, not yours." Tell them this often enough and firmly enough so they will understand and finally believe it.

(7)
The Right to Adequate Time with Both Parents to Establish and Maintain Life-Long, Meaningful Relationships.

It is essential for the children's good mental health to continue a strong, loving relationship with both parents throughout all of their developmental phases. Identifications from early childhood are often not adequate to sustain children for the rest of their lives.

For example, a two-year-old boy whose father leaves the home has not had sufficient time to form an adequate masculine identification and may have difficulty developing one, particularly if he lives in a household composed only of women — with a mother, aunt, grandmother, or a mother's girlfriends. Boys need strong male figures with whom they can identify in order to establish their own masculinity.

The father's role in his daughter's development is just as vital. Girls learn to relate to males in part through their relationship with their fathers. A close, loving relationship with a father helps to prepare a girl for a happy, long-lasting, stable marriage with a suitable marriage partner.

When a parent moves away after a separation or a divorce, it is essential to find adequate father-substitutes or mother-substitutes who can assist in their development. Grandfathers, grandmothers, uncles, aunts, and neighbors are excellent sources, as are people from groups — such as Big Brothers/Sisters, Cub Scouts and Boy Scouts, Brownies and Girl Scouts, sports team coaches, and friends from a church or synagogue. However, I want to make it very clear: There is no true substitute for a child's good relationship with his or her own mother or father.

It is very important that parents allow and encourage each other to be equally involved in all their children's activities. Whether it be Scouting, church, or sports, etc., your children should always see that they have two interested and involved parents.

When one of the parents moves to a distant state, it is vital for that parent to arrange specific times to talk with the children by phone in order to maintain contact with them. It is important to have a planned time schedule for telephoning so children know when to expect calls. They should never have to feel the anxiety of waiting for a call and the disappointment when one does not come.

Other means of keeping in close contact include the use of letters, e-mail, and occasional tape-recorded messages or videotapes of the distant parent's activities. It is very important for a distant parent to always remember the children's birthdays and special holidays to avoid having the children feel that they have been abandoned.

(8)
The Right to Have Frequent and Private Phone Access to Either Parent.

Children have the right to ready access to either parent by telephone without interference from the other parent or other people. They may have urgent needs to speak to their parents often — every day if possible — in order to know that they are cared for and loved, or to be sure that the absent parent is all right.

Out of resentment, angry mothers, fathers, and relatives might try to prevent the children from phoning and receiving telephone calls from the other parent. Sometimes when the other parent calls, the people who answer the phone will make false excuses, saying that the child isn't at home, is asleep, or is too busy to come to the phone.

Some parents set up a telephone "spy" system. They

eavesdrop during phone calls between the child and the other parent and even record the phone conversations.

Some children are not allowed to phone the other parent when they want to. They have to wait until the parent they are living with is not at home. When they secretly phone from home, children call collect so those calls won't show up on the telephone bill.

Other children have to sneak next door or to a friend's house to call a parent, or they use a public pay phone. That's a terrible situation for a child! Such imposed restrictions teach children to be deceptive and can set a pattern for deceptive behavior in their present and future lives. Such unfortunate episodes only tend to teach children to use deception in their own lives.

Some vindictive parents go so far as to change their phone numbers and have them unlisted. Other parents resort to kidnapping the children and moving away without leaving a forwarding address or phone number. Such behavior by the adults deprives their children of the right to love both parents and to have ongoing contact with them.

(9)
The Right to Get Angry with Their Parents.

This right may seem a strange one, but it is a necessary one. If a child becomes angry and says to a parent, "I hate you for getting a divorce!", the parent should not overreact. In all human relationships, everyone has mixed feelings about the people they love. Parents may become angry with their children, but can still love them. Children also can become angry with their parents, but can still love them.

When a child says, "I hate you!", parents should try to remain calm and counter by saying something like, "I understand that you are angry with me. That's okay. I sometimes get angry with my parents, too, but I still love them." Such a response will help the child to calm down and talk about what is behind the outburst.

(10)
The Right to Have Time to Feel Sad about the Divorce.

A divorce can seem like a death in the family. Children need to be allowed to express their grief about that divorce. Unexpressed feelings of grief invariably lead to emotional problems which may include psychosomatic symptoms, depression, or disturbed behavior.

(11)
The Right to Ask Questions about the Divorce and to Express Their Feelings.

Children have the right to be treated with dignity and respect. They should be allowed to ask questions about the divorce. They should be encouraged to express their feelings of sadness, fear, anger, resentment, and joy without having the fear of being rejected.

(12)
The Right to be Praised for Good Things.

Although young people need praise in order to develop a healthy self esteem and confidence, it is sad to say that the average American family uses ten negative words to one, single positive word with their children.

Especially during their parents' divorce, the children's self-esteem and self-worth can be undermined by negative criticism. To counter this problem, children should be given frequent recognition for their good qualities and an abundance of praise for their accomplishments. Negative criticism of their mistakes compounds their loss of self-esteem and should be kept to an absolute minimum.

When children misbehave, parents should tell them that they love them, but they do not like what they did. Giving them a hug and reassuring them that you love them and understand their feelings will have a far more positive effect on their behavior than spanking them or yelling at them.

(13)
The Right Not to be Called
Demeaning and Negative Names.

Some parents, relatives, and caretakers constantly "put down" children by calling them things such as "stupid", "dummy", "fatso", "no-good", "sloppy", "mean", "bad".

They often add insult to injury by including critical comments about the other parent. "You're just like your no-good father", or "You're as mean as your mother". Comments like these not only cut at the child, but they keep emphasizing negative thoughts about the other parent.

(14)
The Right to be a Child and to be
Himself or Herself.

It is unfortunate when a single parent expects his or her child to take on an adult role and fill the shoes of the absent parent. Sometimes a mother will tell her son, "Now, you are the man of the house." Or, a father will tell his daughter, "Now, you are the woman of the house." Don't tell your children either of these things. Such comments place unnecessary burdens on the youngsters.

Children should be allowed to be and act their age and not be pushed into early maturity or into assuming responsibilities beyond their capacity.

After their spouse has left them, some lonely single parents tend to "smother" their children with attention in an attempt to satisfy their own feelings of failure and loss. Children should not be expected to fulfill a parent's emotional needs.

On the other hand, single parents may unconsciously identify their child with their ex-spouse and vent their anger and resentment toward the child. This results in a negative relationship between the parent and the child which can cause lasting damage to the child's self-image.

(15)
The Right to be Taught to Treat Their Parents and Others with Respect and Courtesy.

Most people don't like rude, inconsiderate, or ungrateful children. If you want other people to like your children, then teach your youngsters good manners and show them how to be polite, respectful, and courteous.

The best way for adults to teach children to be polite and courteous is by example. When the people with whom they live show respect and courtesy to each other and to their children, they will find that their children will follow suit and become respectful and courteous, too.

(16)
The Right to Have Predictable Schedules.

When time-sharing schedules are made, the children should be informed of them so they can feel confident that they will have continued contact with both parents.

Small children can be given a calendar to hang on their wall, showing the days they are to spend with each parent clearly marked with a colored marker. Marked calendars for older children are good, too, but also give them schedules in writing, so they can coordinate the visits when making their social plans. More flexibility is usually necessary with older children because they are likely to be involved in sports programs or other organizational activities. Parents should not force their children to miss participating in important events and activities.

(17)
The Right to Have Advanced Warning of Changes in Plans for Spending Time with the Other Parent.

There is nothing more undermining to a child's self-esteem than being dressed, packed, and ready to go to spend time with Mom or Dad, and then having to sit there for hours, waiting for a parent who never shows up. Such thoughtlessness is extremely cruel, hurtful, and damaging to the child.

The ability to trust people comes from experiences in childhood of being able to trust one's parents and to know that they are reliable and will keep their word.

When it is necessary for a parent to postpone or cancel a visit, it is important to give the children advance warning. If something unexpected happens, be sure to telephone your child and explain why you are going to be late or why you must postpone or cancel the visit.

Children have the right to plan for and count on regular times with each parent. However, some flexibility in scheduling should be allowed. It is important for the parents to be able to adjust shared time schedules when their children have important events in their lives. It is also important that children understand that parents may have unexpected emergencies which can force them to alter their plans.

(18)
The Right to Know the Reason for Canceled Visits.

Always tell your children why you are canceling a visit. Above all — tell the truth! It is better to tell the truth than to have your children learn later that you lied.

(19)
The Right to Privacy, Especially in Regard to What Happens During the Time with the Other Parent.

Children should be allowed to enjoy time with the other parent without having to account for everything that happens during the visits.

Parents should not be too intrusive and give children "the third degree" about what occurred. This undermines their freedom to openly relate what they wish to tell. They may resort to lying in order to hide what they don't wish to reveal.

If a child comes home happy from a visit, and the other parent harbors contempt for the ex-spouse, the child will learn to bury his or her good feelings. This erodes the child's happiness.

If youngsters feel they are being forced into pretending that they don't like spending time with the other parent, the children will be cheated out of the happiness they should experience and the pleasant memories they are entitled to.

(20)
The Right to Firm, but Kind and Consistent Behavioral Limits and Discipline in Both Parents' Homes.

Children are not born with the capacity to set limits on their own behavior. They must acquire this through careful, consistent limit-setting by those adults with whom they live. When there are parental differences in handling children's behavior, the children tend to develop behavioral problems.

When parents separate and divorce, it is essential for them to agree on reasonable limits, restrictions, and consequences set for the children. Then both parents should stick to what they have agreed upon. Consistency between the parents is crucial for their children's good behavior.

(21)
The Right to Have the Same Rules Set and Followed in Both Parents' Homes.

Together, both parents should set the same rules for basic procedures and responsibilities. When these rules are consistently followed at both parents' houses, the children know what their parents expect of them.

If the children are to be in bed at a certain time, then bedtime should be the same at both houses. If children are expected to help with the dishes, make their own beds, and use polite table manners at their father's house, they should also do these things at the mother's house.

It is important that children know the rules and understand that both of their parents have the right to set rules and enforce them. If the children break the rules, both parents have the right to discipline them. If this discipline is fair and just, children learn to respect it. If the discipline is too severe or unjust, children will resent it.

Of course, both parents should always stress the rules for safety requirements. For example: Children should not be allowed to play with matches, ride bikes or skateboards in the street in the dark, or play with real guns, knives, and other dangerous objects.

If you strongly disagree with a rule set by the other parent, try to talk to him or her about it — in a friendly, sincere manner, of course — and try to resolve the matter peacefully and fairly, but not in front of the children.

Parents working together and setting reasonable, consistent limits and discipline can help deter their children from developing loyalty conflicts and behavior problems.

(22)
The Right to Respect the Authority of Both Parents.

One parent should never undermine the authority of the other parent. Never tell your children that they do not have to obey the other parent, or that they can break the rules if and when they want to, or that they can be disrespectful toward the other parent.

Let your children know upfront that you will not stand for such actions and that you will back the other parent one hundred percent.

(23)
The Right to Firm, but Kind and Consistent Behavioral Limits and Discipline When They Are with Grandparents and Relatives.

In terms of discipline and behavioral limits, children must be shown a united front by all of the adults who take care of them. This is particularly true with grandparents. It is vital for grandparents to adhere to the behavior limits and forms of discipline that the parents have set. If grandparents let children do things they are not allowed to do at home, this can lead to difficulties in their behavior.

It is very important that both parents make this clear to the grandparents and that the grandparents agree to follow the rules set by the parents.

(24)
The Right to Firm, but Kind and Consistent Behavior Limits and Discipline When They Are with Day-Care Staff, Baby Sitters, and Other Caretakers.

Since many fathers and mothers both work, there are a great many children in some kind of alternate care during the day. To avoid having children develop loyalty conflicts and behavioral problems, it is essential that all caretakers agree to follow the behavioral limits and forms of discipline prescribed by the parents,

For example: Caretakers should make sure youngsters take their baths and go to bed on time; never use abusive discipline or language with the children; and monitor the types of television programs the children are allowed to watch.

Children frequently tell me that they much prefer to have

"Suzy" stay with them because "Suzy" lets them stay up late and watch anything they want on television, even R-rated movies! This should not be tolerated! "Good-bye, Suzy!"

(25)
The Right to Have Both Parents Communicate with Each Other in a Friendly, Congenial, and Courteous Manner.

Children are very impressionable. They learn to behave by copying the actions of those with whom they live. If parents speak to each other in an angry, gruff, and unpleasant manner, the children learn to communicate that way with their siblings, their peers, and others. If these inappropriate communication patterns persist, they often carry forward into the children's adult lives and set the stage for disturbed marital relationships of their own.

If parents don't want their children to suffer the same kinds of distress that they have experienced in their own marriage, they must learn to forgive and forget. It is vital for parents to resolve their differences and settle the issues in a friendly and courteous way. They should learn to be civil with one another for their own good and for the sake of their children.

(26)
The Right to Have Either Parent Pick Up and Deliver a Child in a Peaceful Atmosphere with Friendly, Congenial, and Courteous Parents.

On occasions, I have heard sad stories about fathers coming to pick up their children for a visit. The scenarios may unfold like this: Dad doesn't bother to get out of the car and walk to the door. Instead, he toots the horn and waits for the children to come outside. If he is kept waiting for a few minutes, he becomes angry with Mother and blames her for the delay. He doesn't consider that the child may have stopped to go to the bathroom or wasn't quite ready on time. Instead of being patient, Dad starts yelling and shaking his fists. Sometimes he drives off, leaving the children standing in the yard crying.

Or, the mother drives up to the father's house, lets the children out of the car, and leaves without saying a word to her ex-spouse. She doesn't exercise the courtesy or wisdom to wait long enough to see if her children are safely inside.

Or, during pick-ups and deliveries of the children, the mother or father makes a habit of coming to the door and starting loud arguments in the presence of their children. Children soon begin to dread these times. After witnessing these intolerable scenes, they frequently develop psychosomatic symptoms, such as intestinal upsets or headaches.

If there is a tendency to family violence, children should be protected from the chance of exposure to upsetting episodes. A neutral setting where children can be dropped off and picked up for transition between their parents, such as "The Kids' Exchange", can be utilized in these difficult situations.

Both parents should do everything they can to make the pick-ups and deliveries of children a pleasant, friendly, and positive experience.

(27)
The Right to Peaceful Transitions between Households.

One would think that transporting clothing, toys, schoolbooks, notebooks, and other belongings from one house to another would be a simple, uncomplicated task. Wrong! This often becomes an enormous problem. If a child returns home without all of his or her clothing, it may trigger a parental tirade that could lead to "World War Three!"

Some disgruntled parents will call up and scream, "Where is his jacket?" Or, "Where is her homework assignment?" Or, "You know he can't go to sleep without his teddy bear!"

It would seem reasonable that a truce could be called and the problems of personal attire and belongings could be worked out peacefully. But, no, the tirades continue and may even escalate, week by week. Rarely do these situations have much to do with clothing, toys, or other belongings per se. Usually, these problems really represent the unfinished business of the divorce. The transitions between households simply give the ex-spouses opportunities to continue to argue and complain.

The "paper divorce" may have been finalized. But, the "emotional divorce" may be dragged on for long periods of time as the parents leap at the least provocation to express their resentment through their children.

If parents can resolve their bitterness, they can work together more comfortably to solve the problems of the children's necessary clothing and toys, and anything else. If they can't, they will waste a lot of time in arguments and create a lot of emotional distress for themselves and for their children who deserve better treatment.

(28)
The Right to Have Their Parents Communicate Directly with Each Other, Instead of Using Children as Go-betweens.

Direct communication between parents is a vitally important children's right. Unfortunately, this right tends to be overlooked in many separated and divorced families. Parents who don't want to talk to each other sometimes instruct their children to give the other parent a verbal message. This invariably leads to trouble because children can't always be relied upon to remember to deliver the message. And even when they do remember, the message may become garbled and inaccurate in the telling.

Rather than sending verbal messages with children, it is better to learn to communicate directly with each other, either by telephone or in person, so the child is not caught between the parents.

If you really can't or won't talk to your ex-spouse, then send a written message. But if you are having your child deliver it, make sure the message is friendly and courteous. Never send a threatening or nasty note with your child. That is a terrible, inexcusable thing to do to a child! It is particularly important that parents do not send children back and forth with messages about support payments or legal problems.

(29)
The Right to Tell about
Good Experiences or Unpleasant Experiences
without Fear of Reprisal from Either Parent.

Unfortunately, some parents cannot tolerate their children having a good time with the other parent and may not allow the children to talk about what has happened. This sad situation is emotionally harmful to youngsters.

Children have a right to love both parents and to enjoy being with them, and they should be allowed to talk about the fun they had without the other parent becoming jealous or infuriated.

Children should also feel free to talk about an unpleasant experience while spending time with one parent without the other parent blowing it out of proportion. Use restraint and reason in evaluating the child's explanation of the event.

There are ups and downs in a child's relationships with both parents. Keep in mind that every minute with either parent will not be brimming with pleasure or absolute compatibility.

The fact is, children should be allowed to talk about anything they want to tell you. If a parent limits what a child can tell, important and meaningful information and open communication will be lost, and some basic facts may even become garbled or obscured.

(30)
The Right Not to Hear One Parent Demean or "Bad-Mouth" the Other Parent.

In a divorce situation, it is upsetting for children to hear one parent say hostile or degrading things about the other parent. No matter how much difficulty there has been in the marriage, the child loves both parents.

When a mother criticizes the father, she undermines the child's feelings toward the father. When a father instructs a child to "Tell your mother to stop threatening me or I'll leave town for good!", he undermines the child's feelings for the mother.

Threats frighten children because they are afraid their parents will really do these things. They fear that they will lose one or both of their parents forever.

Both parents must avoid exposing their children to such distressing behavior. It can be avoided easily. Just stop doing it!

(31)
The Right Not to Hear Relatives and Others Demean or "Bad-Mouth" Either Parent.

Grandparents, aunts, uncles, and other relatives, and friends may become angry with one of the parents and start saying unfriendly and unpleasant things in front of the children.

They should not do that. It is just as painful for the children to hear relatives and friends say awful things about their parents as it is to have their parents criticize each other. Such unkind actions are hurtful to children. Stop doing it!

(32)
The Right to Love and be Loved by Both Sets of Grandparents and Other Relatives.

Children need to belong to a family and to know about their "roots". Continuity of family relationships with the older generation helps to strengthen the children's sense of security and self-worth and goes a long way in making up for some of what they have lost in a broken family.

Following a divorce, if both sets of grandparents remain friendly with both parents, they have a better chance of maintaining a good relationship with the children. When the animosity is severe between one side of the family and the other, the children can be cut off from one set of grandparents and other family members. When this happens, a tremendous source of emotional support and stability is lost in the lives of the youngsters. Close relationships may never be regained.

Children often sadly tell me about not being able to see their grandparents, uncles, aunts, and their favorite cousins. They sometimes conclude that these relatives don't like them anymore, and they grieve for their loss of contact with these people. What is even more heartbreaking, the children frequently blame themselves for the estrangement.

Like it or not, if grandparents and relatives want to maintain a good relationship with the children, they may have to swallow their pride and their hurt feelings toward the ex-daughter-in-law or son-in-law. This may be difficult to do, but

it can be worth whatever effort it takes. Do everything possible
to keep in touch and stay in the hearts of the children you love.

(33)
The Right to Life-Long Relationships with Step-Parents, Grandparents, Siblings, and Other Extended Family Members.

It is also important for children to be allowed to continue
to have life-long relationships with all of their extended family members, including step-parents, siblings, grandparents,
aunts, uncles, cousins, and friends. Continuity of a complete
family offers a sense of belonging. It is very unfair and unjust
to cut children off from any part of their families.

After the divorce and re-marriages of one or both parents,
tension often arises when parents struggle to decide with
whose family the children will be allowed to celebrate holidays,
such as Halloween, Thanksgiving, Hanukkah, Christmas, and
Easter. They need to be very fair, flexible, and cooperative in
arranging to take turns in having the children for holidays,
instead of arguing and contacting lawyers to settle matters.

(34)
The Right to Have Both Parents, and Their Relatives and Friends Attend School Functions, Athletic Games, Graduations, Birthday Parties, Weddings, and Other Significant Events in a Peaceful Atmosphere.

Children want both of their parents, and their relatives
and friends to be present at special functions and events.
They want everyone who attends to be friendly and pleasant

so everyone can have a good time.

It is painful and distressing for children to have their parents come to a school or other event and have them interact in an unpleasant, rude manner. I have frequently heard about episodes when both parents, the step-parents, relatives, or family friends have gone to a child's sports event and ended up yelling at each other about child support or some other contentious issue. This is terribly embarrassing for the children to witness in front of their friends, teachers, and others.

Divorced parents can avoid a lifetime of family discord and misery if they will reconcile their differences. Otherwise, these feuding parents may not be welcome at special events in their children's lives and even in their grandchildren's lives. If you can't forgive and forget, at least be civil with one another so everyone in the family, especially your children, can enjoy special occasions.

(35)
The Right to Have Proper Physical and Mental Health Care, Including Adequate Health Insurance.

In many separated and divorced families, issues involving money become a major focus of tremendous tension and conflict. A common question that arises is who will pay for the children's health care and insurance. Frequently, the divorce decree will stipulate who is to maintain the insurance, but if the responsible parent fails to meet this obligation, the children are left without adequate medical coverage.

To avoid tragedies from delays in obtaining prompt emergency treatment for a child's illness or injury, it is absolutely imperative that adequate medical insurance coverage be maintained for children's health needs and that both parents are informed about insurance policies.

(36)
The Right to Have Both Parents Permitted Access to Medical, Dental, and All Other Types of Health Records.

It is essential for both parents to be fully aware of any medical or dental problems their children may have so they can assist in obtaining any required treatments. Failure to share medical information and to inform the other parent about any necessary medications and treatments can lead to disruptive situations while a child is with the other parent.

Both parents should be interested in their children's health. However, it is not uncommon for one parent to attempt to prevent an ex-spouse from having access to a child's medical and dental records. Why do they do this? Out of jealousy, bitterness, anger, and resentment. But it doesn't make good sense because <u>both</u> parents must be informed in order to protect the children.

Unfortunately, some parents may disagree and squabble over the children's medical treatment or which doctor or dentist to use. This is particularly true when a youngster requires psychiatric or psychological treatment. An objection may arise when one parent fears that such treatment might reveal things that could be used against him or her and adversely affect the frequency or length of time with their child, or even affect the custody of the child.

(37)
The Right to Therapy or Counseling if Distress or Symptoms Persist.

When children show symptoms of being emotionally upset or have persistent worries, concerns, or symptoms during and/or after a divorce, they have the right to receive therapy or counseling.

Unfortunately, parents who are suspicious that a request for treatment of a child might be a ploy to attempt to begin another round of litigation to change custody or time-sharing may resist getting professional help for the child. This often interferes with a child's right to have appropriate help early enough before the problems become so entrenched that they may be resistive to therapeutic intervention

Most children going through the painful process of family disintegration could use some short term, individualized help in coping with the stress they experience. For others, group therapy could be very useful. Some school counselors offer divorce group counseling in their schools.

At the outset of therapy, parental fears can be relieved if the child's therapist makes it quite clear to both of the parents and to the child that there will be absolutely no testimony or litigation connected with the therapeutic work. A written agreement to this effect should be signed by the therapist and by both parents. This is important because it takes away the threats to the child and the therapist that they could become embroiled in any future legal disagreements or court battles.

(38)
The Right to Have Both Parents Permitted Access to School Records.

It is essential for both parents to be fully aware of any school problems that their children may be having so they can assist their youngsters with their homework or whatever is needed.

It is also important that both parents are aware of their children's interests and achievements in school.

(39)
The Right to Have Adequate Housing,
Clothing, Nourishment, and Other Essentials.

In many divorces, disputes about housing, clothing, food, and other essentials can erupt and create chronic struggles between the parents.

The fact is, every parent knows that their children grow out of shoes and clothing. And like it or not, today's children are very fad conscious and peer oriented in selecting clothing. What brand tags are popular? What styles are "in"? What colors are "out"? And some, who think that new is better if it looks old, want their clothing to be discolored, ragged, and oversized.

At this point, I would really like to stress how important it is to encourage your children to see and be with the other parent as much as possible. The more the other parent sees the children and is involved with them, the more he or she is apt to want to help them obtain needed clothing and other essentials.

Housing is another focal point for parental battles. If the mother retains the family house, the father may have to rent an apartment, which may not be as pleasant or spacious. That often leads to more hard feelings and resentment by the parent who resides in the smaller or more meagerly furnished place.

Sometimes children tell me that when visiting Dad's apartment, they have to sleep on a mattress on the floor, because there are not enough beds. Or they will say that the furnishings at Mom's house are not as nice or comfortable as those at Dad's house.

Adequate food also may be a point of contention when a divorced parent with a lowered income has difficulty supplying the children with enough to eat. Children have a right to adequate nourishment. Both parents are responsible to see that this need is met, not just the one with the bigger house, or the newer car, or the higher income — but both parents.

If Mom doesn't have enough money to purchase

necessary food for the children —"Hey, Dad, how about some help!" Or if Dad is without enough money — Mom should help him buy groceries for the children!

(40)
The Right to Prompt Payment of Child Support and the Avoidance of Threats of Jail for Either Parent.

One of the most contentious aspects for some divorcing families is the question of child support — how much, and who should pay – which becomes the focus of endless debates and often litigation. More ill feelings seem to be generated by the subject of child support than almost any other issue.

It can be tremendously traumatic for children to hear one parent make threats of having the other parent arrested because of non-payment of child support. To have either parent sent to jail directly interferes with the child's right to regular contact with his or her parent. It can also be demeaning and frightening for a child to know that a parent is in jail. Moreover, if an ex-spouse is in jail, there is no possibility of earning money with which to make the payments.

As parents, it is your responsibility to help support your children. Child support payments should always be made on time because the money is needed to buy necessities. And you should want to avoid the threat of spending time in jail.

(41)
The Right to Protection from Abandonment or Neglect.

Parents should protect and care for their children, not only because they are supposed to, but because they want to. One would hope that the love parents have for their children would keep them diligent in trying to make sure their young-sters are safe at all times.

Young children need protection, care, and constant supervision, and they should never be left alone!

Nevertheless, little children tell me about being left alone at night while their parent goes out on a date or to a bar. Being left alone can be very frightening to young children. They will inevitably feel abandoned, and they may develop emotional difficulties.

Besides, it is not safe for children to be left alone. News broadcasts report about children being injured or burned to death in fires when no one was at home. Abandonment in which children have been left alone for days at a time has also been reported to the Child Protective Services. Sometimes these neglected children are taken from their parents and placed in other homes, and rightfully so!

Older children and teenagers must also be properly supervised. Parents must know where these children are and what they are doing. They must know how much they can trust them. Parents must keep close tabs on their children's activities without appearing to become jailers or wardens.

Talk to your older children and teenagers. Listen to them without constantly interrupting them. Set firm guidelines for them to follow. You are responsible for your children. Take care of them!

(42)
The Right Not to be Allowed
to Manipulate Either Parent.

Do your children a great big favor: Do not allow them to manipulate you. They may try to convince you that "Dad always lets us watch this television program when we're at his house!" Or, "Mom lets us stay out after midnight!" Or, "Dad always lets us eat all the candy we want!"

Either parent could forestall such attempts to manipulate by not giving in to the children just to placate them. Instead, one might say, "Let's call your father (or mother) and discuss it." Such a response may solve the problem immediately.

(43)
The Right Not to be Manipulated by Either Parent.

Using children as pawns in the emotional struggles that go on between separated or divorced parents is frightfully damaging and difficult for children to endure.

Parents may try to manipulate their children by saying such things as, "If you don't tell your father that I'm planning to take him back to court for more child support money, I'll buy you a toy"; or "If you won't tell your mother that we went over to my girlfriend's house, I'll take you to the circus next week."

Never try to bribe your children to lie or conceal the truth. Such unhealthy manipulation causes great distress for children. Not only does it put them in the middle between their parents, it also teaches children to think that it is okay to tell lies and side with one parent against the other.

(44)
The Right Not to be Bribed by Over-Gifting.

In several families with which I have worked, one of the parents tried to bribe their children by giving them expensive gifts. These manipulating parents hoped the gifts would pursuade the children to side with them in their ongoing custody battles.

One striking example occurred in a long, drawn-out custody dispute that went on for years. The father offered to buy his teen-aged son a car in an effort to induce him to say that he wanted to file a petition to live with his father. The father's real motivations were to stop making child support payments to his ex-wife and let her experience the pain of having her son choose to live with his father.

This manipulation led to a tremendous loyalty conflict for the teenager. The boy felt helplessly trapped between his warring parents. He wanted to live with his mother, but he also wanted that car.

I have also heard about grandparents and other relatives who showered gifts upon the children. Their motives are usually poor because they are trying to gain favoritism with the children and win allegiance to their point of view.

And by the way, try not to fall into the trap of feeling you have to stage lavish or duplicate birthday parties — one at Mom's house and one at Dad's. Whenever possible, it would be best to plan such celebrations together and give them together. The same goes for major holidays. Make these occasions normal family gatherings that provide your children with consistent traditions and experiences.

The bottom line, though, is that any kind of manipulation by over-gifting children should be avoided. It is not fair to the children. It can tempt them to make wrong decisions in order to get material things they want.

(45)
The Right Not to be Involved in any Plot Devised by One Parent against Another.

Remember — Your children do not want to lose or upset either parent. Never try to involve them in plots against the other parent.

In an effort to have time-sharing curtailed, a parent may attempt to get a child to accuse the other parent of mistreating him or her. Do not encourage your child to do that! It is a very poor tactic that could have disastrous psychological consequences. Never suggest or encourage your child to tell a lie about anything or anyone!

(46)
The Right to be Protected from Parental Drunkenness and Spousal Abuse between the Adults.

Your children should be protected at all times from parental drunkenness and witnessing of spousal abuse!

Drunkenness on the part of either parent has devastating effects on children. Parents who are drunk should not visit their children. Most often, spousal abuse tends to occur when there has been heavy drinking on the part of one or both parents. Under the influence of alcohol, parents become less attentive to their children and are more prone to neglect, abuse, and abandon them. It is frightening and very traumatic for children to see and hear either of their parents in a drunken, abusive state.

In working with adult patients, it has become clear to me that many of their distressing symptoms are related to their own childhood experiences in a family setting where there was drunkenness and physical abuse. People may carry the scars of such damaging parental behavior throughout their lives and may require prolonged therapy to overcome its effects.

If the father is harsh, punishing, or an abusive alcoholic, frequently his daughters tend to seek a succession of abusive or alcoholic partners. Sons may become abusive fathers and husbands themselves.

If the adults cannot stop their use of alcohol, they should

seek help immediately. There are many sources of help available, including Alcoholics Anonymous. If you are an alcoholic — get help — if not to save yourself, then to save your children.

There are community resources such as shelters for battered women and children that can offer a haven from abusive situations. If the abuse persists, Child Protective Services can be contacted for help.

(47)
The Right to be Protected from Parents Who Use Drugs.

Your children should never have to endure or be with a drug-addicted parent!

As with alcoholism, the use of drugs by parents can be very damaging for children. While under the influence of drugs, adults are also likely to become less attentive to the children and are more likely to neglect, abuse, or abandon them.

There is no doubt that drug use by parents has a significant influence on children because youngsters tend to copy what they see their parents do. When talking with drug-addicted adolescents, they very often tell me that they had their start with drug use from observing their parents' drug habits. It may be difficult to believe, but adults frequently allow children to share in taking their drugs, thus promoting drug use in the young people. If you are addicted to drugs and cannot stop using them on your own, seek help — the sooner, the better!

(48)
The Right to Protection from Physical Abuse.

Children have an absolute right to be protected from all forms of physical abuse. Sometimes, after a destructive marriage, especially with an alcoholic or drug-addicted parent, children may be physically abused by that parent during time-sharing. It is the legal duty of the other parent and all professional people — teachers, nurses, physicians, social workers, and others — to report to the authorities any evidence of physical abuse. Any signs of bruises, belt marks, burns, or other physical signs of abuse should be reported promptly.

Unfortunately, abuse is not always easy to detect because much of it occurs when a responsible person is not with the children. There are many "latch-key kids", who are home alone after school without any proper adult supervision. This allows youngsters many opportunities to suffer various types of abuse — from brothers or sisters, other relatives, neighbors, and even strangers.

Early in their lives, your children need adequate training regarding how to avoid physical abuse from relatives, friends, acquaintances, or strangers. Your children should also understand and be encouraged to tell you immediately if they have been abused by anyone!

(49)
The Right to Protection from Emotional Abuse.

As with physical abuse, emotional abuse may occur in a variety of forms and from various people — parents, grandparents, relatives, caretakers, neighbors, even teachers. Name-calling, belittling, teasing, and frightening children are forms of emotional abuse that are cruel and damaging to the youngsters' self-esteem and self-assurance.

Children must be treated with respect and offered a lot of encouragement in order for them to develop and maintain healthy emotional attitudes.

(50)
The Right to Protection from
Sexual Abuse.

The number of incidences of sexual abuse of children has increased dramatically in recent years. There are many contributing factors which include the sexual revolution, the availability of explicit and sexually stimulating material on television, videotapes, and the Internet, and in the movies, as well as in magazines and books. The lessening of parental guidance and supervision also has contributed to a loosening and lowering of moral standards about sexual conduct.

Teen-age pregnancy rates have risen dramatically, and an epidemic of adolescent HIV infections and venereal diseases makes it strikingly evident that sexual behavior among young people is extremely common.

Children are abused by a variety of people, many of whom we think we should be able to trust. Sexual abusers may include parents, step-parents, siblings, cousins, uncles, aunts, and sometimes even grandparents, church youth workers, priests, camp counselors, day-care workers, teachers, coaches, baby sitters, and almost anyone else who has an opportunity to spend time alone with children.

Historically, parents seemed to think that girls were more vulnerable and should be protected from predators and that boys could take care of themselves. But that's not true. Boys can be just as vulnerable and must be protected, too!

Alcoholism and drug addiction on the part of the adults pose additional threats to children. Both alcohol and drugs tend to remove inhibitions and dull one's sense of right and wrong, which can lead to people's doing things that they would not do otherwise

Parents must be constantly vigilant in protecting their children. Those unfortunate children who are abused will often bear emotional scars for the rest of their lives.

(51)
The Right to be Warned about
Sexual Predators.

Children must be given adequate information and be prepared to tell someone if they have been sexually abused.

From early ages, both boys and girls should be taught to <u>immediately</u> tell their parents, teachers, or other trusted adults of any attempts by <u>anyone</u> to inappropriately touch their bodies — whether those persons are relatives, friends, baby sitters, neighbors, or strangers.

Your children must be assured that you or another trusted adult will listen to them and believe them when they tell. They must not be allowed to feel that they have to keep such things to themselves because they feel ashamed or guilty.

Parents should use great care in evaluating the people with whom they entrust their children! If you suspect or discover that your child has been sexually abused, you are morally bound to keep your children away from such people and legally bound to report the perpetrators.

(52)
The Right Never to Have One Parent Falsely
Accuse the Other Parent
of Sexual, Physical, or Emotional Abuse.

Sometimes vindictive parents, who want to shut off a child's access to the other parent, will persuade the child to falsely accuse the other parent of some type of abuse — physical, emotional, or sexual. This can be extremely damaging to a youngster since the child is being asked to make false accusations against a parent.

Some parents even go "shopping" for a professional per-

son to support such allegations in a court battle in an attempt
to restrict their ex-spouse's time-sharing rights or custody of
the children. I am sorry to say that there are some profes-
sionals who do get taken in by persuasive parents and then
don't fully investigate the charges.

Besmirching an ex-spouse's reputation and honor is a grave
injustice that he or she does not deserve. Above all, no child should
have to endure being made a part of a heinous lie!

Quite frankly, if you tell a lie, you deserve to be caught. But
your children don't deserve it. Learning that a parent is dishonest
can be very upsetting to them. And once your children know that
you have lied, they may never again completely trust you.

Never falsely accuse your ex-spouse of anything!

Never brainwash your children to lie about their other
parent or to lie about anything!

(53)
The Right to Bodily Privacy and to Protest against Inappropriate Touching of Their Bodies and Private Parts.

Children have the right to bodily privacy and protection
against inappropriate touching of their bodies and private
parts. Period. Exclamation point!

(54)
The Right to Bathe Alone.

It is much better for children to bathe alone than it is for
them to bathe with others.

Bathing with an adult can be sexually over-stimulating
for a child. Viewing an adult's genitals can stir up an early

onset in young children of greater sexual curiosity, interest, fantasies, and concerns. Children can also develop feelings of inferiority when they compare themselves with an adult's physical attributes.

My clinical experience with children has shown that it is not only girls who may be sexually abused while bathing. Boys also may be subject to sexual abuse. In a situation where a young boy bathes with his father or step-father, an older brother, or another male who may have gender confusion and identity difficulties, sexually stimulating physical contact may occur. This close bodily contact may lead to the boy's gender confusion as well as to feelings of remorse, shame, and guilt.

Girls who bathe with their mothers or other female adults may similarly become subject to sexual over-stimulation if the adult has gender identity problems and makes excessively close bodily contact with them.

It is also unwise for boys and girls to bathe together. Likewise, girls bathing with girls and boys bathing with boys can become a problem. Based upon comments from the young people I have counseled, all kinds of sexual curiosity and activity started as a result of bathing with their siblings. It is better to allow children to bathe alone and in privacy.

(55)
The Right to Sleep Alone.

Children should not be made to sleep with a mother, a father, or other adults.

Sleeping with adults can be too sexually over-stimulating for children. This may be particularly damaging when a divorced mother living alone insists on sleeping with her son who has taken the place of her husband in her unconscious motivations. The same is true for a little girl becoming her daddy's replacement for the missing mother. This can be true for same sex parents when there are gender identity issues involved. Boys sleeping with brothers or other boys and girls sleeping with sisters or other girls can also lead to problems.

Sometimes parents say their child is afraid to sleep alone, so they allow the child to sleep with them. This may increase a child's fearfulness and dependency needs, and should be gently, but firmly, discouraged. Sleeping alone tends to build self-confidence and independence.

(56)
The Right to Protection from Over-Stimulation by Nudity and Witnessing Overt Adult Sexual Behavior.

It is disturbing that children often tell me about watching their mother or father having sex with another person after the divorce. Such over-stimulation compounds the sexual confusion of children and may lead to early sexual activity by the young people.

Similarly, exposure to nudity in either parent's home can be detrimental to children and should be avoided.

(57)
The Right to be Protected from TV Programs, Videos, Movies, the Internet, and Books That Contain Pornography and Violence.

You want them, you got them — more than seventy channels of television! Some are good; some are bad; some are informative; some are disgusting; some are enlightening;

some are demeaning; some are helpful; and some are damaging! For your children's well being, select the channels and the programs wisely!

Many adults have trouble separating the good from the bad, the uplifting from the degrading. So why would anyone think that children should be allowed to make all of their own selections of programs? They should not be allowed to do this. But many of them are left to pick and chose on their own.

Every day, many unsupervised children are exposed to hours and hours of television. The average child in the United States watches between five and seven hours of television and video games per day, much of which contains material unsuitable for young children. As a result, they inevitably encounter vast amounts of over-stimulating sexual material and violence.

At present, young boys and girls comprise a large part of the audiences for wrestling programs with their inherently violent motifs. Many children become addicted to television wrestling and video games like "Wrestling Mania" which tends to motivate them to imitate the violent behavior.

It is essential to protect young children from these types of programs because they can be detrimental to the healthy emotional development of youngsters.

There is no doubt that children do copy behavior which they see in their homes, and they do emulate the behavior seen on television and in video games. Nursery schools and kindergartens have had to ban children from playing karate, Ninja Turtles, Power Rangers, and Poke'mon in their school settings in order to reduce the aggressive play that children copy from television programs.

In my professional opinion, it is also unwise for young children to have a television set in their own rooms. This can result in exposure to undesirable programs.

Parents and caretakers should carefully monitor what their children watch on television, in video games, and on the Internet, where pornography and violence are rampant.

More child-appropriate programs for young children can be seen on PBS, including Mr. Rogers, Sesame Street, Reading Rainbow, and Barney. These are not likely to stir up aggressive or sexual behavior in the viewers.

Recent research at the University of Pennsylvania Annenberg Public Policy Center on the tremendous impact of television on children, indicates that many parents do not understand the TV rating system, and also that they do not pay attention to what their children are viewing.

Studies reveal that many youngsters who are ten to fifteen years of age say their favorite programs are: Wrestling, The Simpsons, Rugrats, and Dawson's Creek.

The shows most prohibited by parents are: The Jerry Springer Show, MTV Network, South Park, The Simpsons, and shows on the HBO Network.

The television most recommended for children includes: The Learning Channel, Discovery Channel, Touched by an Angel, Seventh Heaven, PBS, Bill Nye, the Science Guy, The History Channel, and The National Geographic shows.

It is my hope that parents will become more aware of the potential damage that unrestricted television access can do to their children and will pay closer attention to their viewing habits.

In addition to the media exposure described above, parents should be aware of the harmful effect on young people of the type of music to which they may be exposed today.

Some of the rap music on radio, audiotapes, and CD's which young people are listening to contain extremely demeaning and foul language. Some defile women, others glorify suicide, or are anti-parental and anti-social in attitude.

Parents should listen to their children's music and use caution in allowing them to buy downgrading types of music or to attend rock concerts of the more offensive bands.

Parents must be responsible! If you care about your children, do all you can to monitor what they see and what they hear.

(58)
The Right to Live in a Smoke-Free Home.

Children who are exposed to second-hand smoke are at risk for the same diseases as those of smokers. If you are addicted to tobacco, make sure that you do not smoke where your children are exposed to it. Be humane and do not pollute the air space of others. Instead, go outdoors to smoke, away from other people, where your smoking will not affect the health of your family members or anyone else.

The fact is, for their own good, parents should not smoke. And they certainly should discourage their children from becoming smokers.

(59)
The Right to be Kept from Hearing Parents' Discussions with Lawyers, Other Professionals, Family Members, or Friends.

This is a very important right! Children in a divorcing family should not be included in nor overhear any of the conversations by either of the parents with lawyers, other professional people, family members, or friends.

Children have absolutely no business entering the offices of lawyers or listening to their parents' discussions about legal matters.

Children have absolutely no business listening to their parents' discussions with therapists.

Children have absolutely no business listening to discussions between their parents, or between their parents and family members or friends, regarding the divorce.

Telephone conversations between their parents and other adults should take place when the children are in school, asleep, playing outside, or away from home.

(60)
The Right to Have Their Parents Settle Their Divorce Promptly.

A divorce is usually very upsetting for everyone involved, not only for parents, but for children, too. If you are going to divorce, settle matters with dispatch, and do so with as much compassion and understanding as possible.

Frequently, the bitterness and resentment at the time of separation persists and interferes with the child's relationship with both parents. Since the bitterness is usually worse during a hotly contested divorce hearing, I encourage parents to try to settle their differences out of court whenever possible. The use of mediation is often less traumatic and less expensive than enduring a long, drawn-out court battle.

Once custody is settled, for the children's security, it should not be subjected to unnecessary changes.

(61)
The Right Not to Have to Testify against Either Parent in Court.

Children should be completely left out of legal disputes between their parents. They should not become pawns in a legal battle. They should not be taken into a courtroom or forced to testify against a parent. It can even make a child feel that he or she is a traitor to one of the parents.

Having children testify against a parent is a potentially disastrous imposition upon a child. It is a damaging, threatening, destructive, unhealthy experience that can emotionally tear that child apart.

To make matters worse, very often a child's testimony has been colored by coercion and tainted by "brainwashing" by one of the parents and does not represent the child's true feelings about the other parent.

If you must have a battle in court, make it one between you and your spouse. Leave the children out of it!

> Note:
> There are some exceptions when a court orders an evaluation of suspected abuse. An attorney or guardian *ad litem* and a court-appointed, impartial professional may be asked to make an evaluation of the allegations. If there are substantially positive findings of abuse, the child may be asked to testify in a trial of the perpetrator. Since this is invariably a very anxiety-producing situation for children, the child has a right to have the roles of the legal and professional people explained. The nature of the litigation should be made clear in age-appropriate words so the youngster can readily understand it.

For children, it is far less traumatic to have them testify in a judge's chambers with both lawyers present, rather than in a courtroom in the presence of the alleged perpetrator. Closed circuit television may be used in these situations.

(62)
The Right Not to be Present When Either Parent is Served with a Subpoena or is Arrested.

Sometimes by chance, a subpoena is handed to a parent in front of the children. That is an awful experience for the parent and the children.

However, some vengeful parents like to try to demean and embarrass their ex-spouse as much as possible. So they purposely plot a time when a process server can serve the legal papers in front of the children.

The time selected may coincide with the time the other parent is picking up or dropping off the children for a scheduled visit. The process server may even hide behind a bush or a tree, and then suddenly jump out, startling the ex-spouse and frightening the children.

An even worse scenario occurs when vengeful parents have "brainwashed" the children to plot with them against the other parent. The children are instructed to encourage the other parent to arrive at a particular time and place so that a process server doesn't have to wait very long.

Either version of such an act is shameful! Being exposed to these kinds of situations can be extremely traumatic to children. Every effort should be made to avoid such incidents!

(63)
The Right to Develop Positive Relationships with People Whom Their Parents Date.

Children should be allowed to like and enjoy the people their divorced parents date. Some parents, spurred by anger, bitterness, or jealousy, have difficulty in encouraging this.

I have heard mothers ask their children if their father is still dating "that awful woman"; and I have heard fathers ask, "Is your mother still dating that jerk?"

While I understand these human urges to lash out in insulting ways, I don't think parents always consider or understand the damage their comments are doing to the children. By telling them not to like certain people, they are putting their children in a terrible position! People whom their parents date may be very nice, friendly, and considerate — good people for the children to meet and know. But because a parent has told the children not to like someone, the children may feel like traitors if they do.

Do not impose these problems on your children. Somehow, you should pull yourself together and rise above the temptation to encourage negative attitudes in your children. Parents often need to be better than they really want to be.

Sometimes children resent and resist their parents' beginning to date other people. They may do their best to drive away the "intruders" by behaving obnoxiously. This should be discouraged by the parent who wishes to form a new relationship. Don't let your children rule your lives!

(64)
The Right to Develop Positive Relationships with New Step-parents, Step-grandparents, Step-siblings, Step-uncles, Step-aunts, and Extended Family Friends.

When one of the parents remarries, the children should be allowed and encouraged to relate freely and in a friendly manner with the new step-parents and other extended family relatives and friends.

This is often difficult for the other parent if he or she has not remarried. The resentment this parent feels should not be passed on to the children. The children should not be told to dislike the step-parent. If they begin to like the step-parent and even call her "Mom" or him "Dad", the children may feel guilty and uncomfortable, especially if these terms of familiarity stir up even more resentment on the part of the other parent.

No matter what, children should be encouraged to form close and loving relationships with their new step-parents, step-siblings, and other step-family members, especially step-grandparents who can be very warm and loving to their step-grandchildren.

Extended family members can add many positive experiences in your children's lives. Give them the opportunity to do so. Don't allow your animosity to cause unnecessary interference.

I am happy to say that some parents handle these situations brilliantly. One youngster recently told me how lucky he was because he now had eight grandparents. Both of his parents had remarried, and he was enjoying relationships with both sets of extended families. He said that he now gets a lot more birthday cards and presents.

That's the way it should be. Encourage your children to like and enjoy members of their extended families.

(65)
The Right to be Taught and Encouraged to Follow Spiritual Beliefs.

As do most human beings, children have spiritual needs that are important to them. They want to believe in something more than the here and now. They want to feel that they are worth more than a walking body and a thinking head.

Children who have spiritual beliefs tend to have a stronger sense of self-esteem and identity. They tend to make friends with peers who have better morals and standards. They tend to join productive, worthwhile groups, rather than destructive ones.

Children who do not have spiritual beliefs are more apt to join anti-social and anti-parental crowds and make friends with troublesome peers. They have a much greater tendency to get hooked on drugs and alcohol and embroiled in gangs that commit criminal acts.

Early in their lives, children should be taught and encouraged to follow the spiritual beliefs of their parents' choice. This requires parents to demonstrate their own faith and spiritual beliefs. Unfortunately, many parents today have few if any spiritual beliefs of their own, so they have nothing to pass on to their children. In my professional opinion, this has contributed greatly to the turmoil and discontent of many young people in America.

Spiritual growth is one of the most important gifts you can nurture in your children. It may also add strength and purpose to your own life.

(66)
The Right to Know Their Rights.

It is important for parents and other adults to consider and observe the rights of their children. It is just as important that children be aware of these rights and be allowed to benefit from them in their day-to-day living.

58

AFTERWORD

Now that both of you parents have read all of your children's rights and have carefully considered each and every one of them, you should be able to start making wiser decisions because they will be based upon these rights. I have no doubt that these decisions will lead to healthier, happier children who will have better opportunities to grow up to become healthier, happier adults.

By keeping your children's rights in mind, the meetings and conversations between the two of you about your children should be more pleasant and constructive. Tensions between you will be reduced, and some of your personal distress should be relieved. And, believe it or not, a new respect for each other can be built. Such an improved relationship will be enormously beneficial to you and your children.

This book is not meant to be a read-it-once, put-it-away kind of book for either parent. The first readings can help the two of you get on track. Later readings can help you stay on track. Every so often, both of you should pick up this book and read it again. In fact, before you make a decision regarding a specific problem, it would be wise if both of you reread the sections that pertain to that problem.

Whatever problems arise, I promise that if both of you consider your children's rights <u>first</u>, you will be able to solve most difficulties.

I strongly suggest that you share this book with all the grandparents and other relatives and caretakers because they are also important in your children's lives. You need to have the grandparents and others be aware of and understand the rights of your children. Their cooperation in respecting those rights is vital to the development of your children's emotional growth and well being.

As responsible parents, you must lead the way by setting proper examples for others to follow. You will find that others will respond in like fashion to the attitudes and actions you display toward each other, your children, your family members, and your friends.

If you are considerate, reasonable, understanding, unselfish, thoughtful, courteous, cooperative, and caring, you stand a good chance of having others become considerate, reasonable, understanding, unselfish, thoughtful, courteous, cooperative, and caring.

I have always found that people who possess these attributes can work out almost anything. In raising your children, you can use all the help you can get.

Remember — you may divorce your spouse, but you can never divorce your children!

The present and future welfare of your children depends upon the care and attention you give to them, the love you express to them, and the wisdom you use in the decisions you make.

As parents, your goal should be to develop emotionally healthy and happy children and transform them into emotionally healthy and happy adults.

I hope this book will help you achieve your goal.